HARNESSING-UP

HARNESSING-UP

Single harness
correct fitting and putting to
pony, horse or donkey

COMPILED BY
Nancy Pethick and Anne Norris

PHOTOGRAPHS BY ELSA MAYO

J. A. Allen
LONDON AND NEW YORK

Published in Great Britain in 1979 by

J. A. Allen & Company Limited

1 Lower Grosvenor Place, London SW1W OEL

and in the USA by

J. A. Allen

Sporting Book Centre Inc., Canaan, N.Y. 12029

ISBN 0-85131-319-1

British Library Cataloguing in Publication Data

Pethick, Nancy

Harnessing-up

1. Draft horses

2. Harness

I. Title II. Norris, Anne

636.1 '4   SF311

ISBN 0-85131-319-1

Printed in Great Britain by Charles Clarke (Haywards Heath) Ltd.

Foreword

In presenting this little booklet we have tried to answer a cry for help from many anxious to take up Driving.

In this modern world, the sight of a pile of leather straps with apparently endless buckles appears a formidable jigsaw puzzle.

If by putting it into picture book form, which anyone can prop up on the stable yard gate, we have helped to ensure that others get even a quarter as much pleasure out of driving a good horse as we have had, then that will be our reward and also, we sincerely hope, some comfort to the animal concerned!

We should also like to express our sincere thanks to Elsa Mayo, Caroline Douglas and Jane Dod, not to mention the Animals, for their assistance and co-operation.

Nancy Pethick
Anne Norris

Full collar for a horse or pony

If you have an Assistant, get them to hold the animal, and use their spare arm as a rest for the harness. Otherwise tie the pony to a ring.

Take off the headcollar and strap it around the pony's neck. Remove the hames from the collar and hang them on the Assistant's arm, or onto a nearby hook or bar.

Ease the collar on the knee.

7

With the collar upside down, put it gently but firmly over the head, taking care not to force it over the eyes.

Place the hames into their groove, and fasten the hame strap firmly.

Twist the collar gently round the narrowest part of the neck, just behind the head.

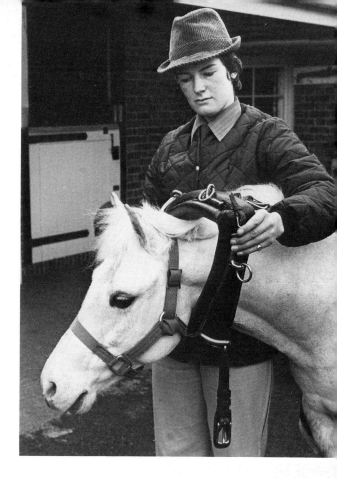

Push the collar back into position against the shoulder.

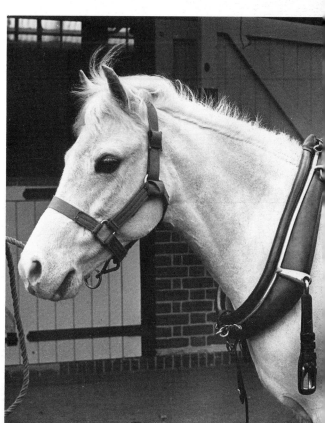

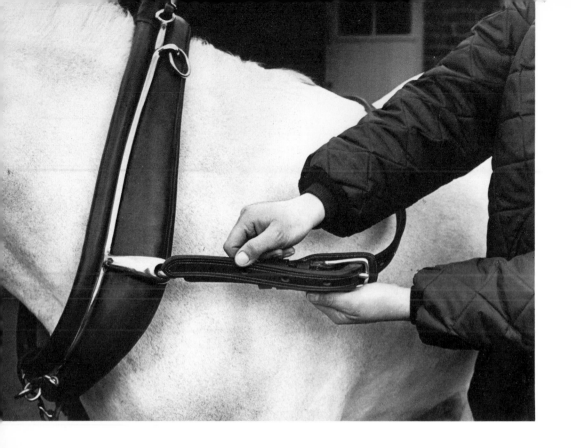

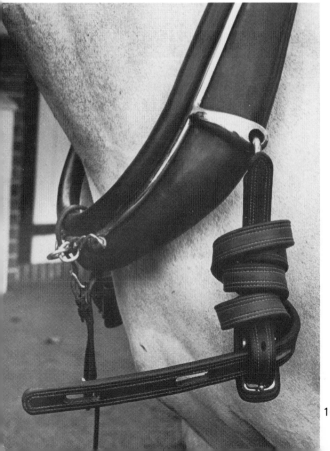

Buckle on the traces, using the holes you know or judge to be required. The point hole should not be used if possible. Twist the trace up twice over the buckle, and pull the free end to prevent the traces falling to the ground.

Full collar for a donkey

A 'split' collar must be used.

Remove the hames from the collar and hang them up.

Undo the top strap on the collar, slip the open collar round the neck, from below, and fasten the strap firmly.

Place the hames into their groove, and fasten with the hame strap. Buckle on the traces, as for the pony.

The headcollar can now be replaced if required.

Breast collar for a horse, pony or donkey

Undo the neck strap. Place the breast strap round the chest, then bring the neck strap over the neck and fasten.

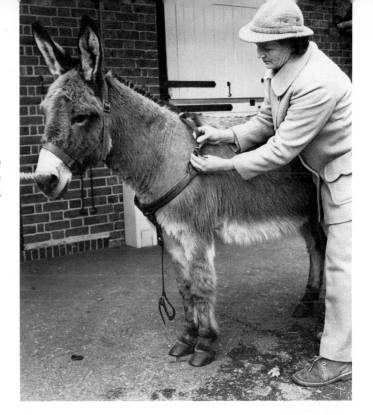

Take care to adjust the height to not less than 1in. above the point of the shoulder, and below the windpipe.

Put on the traces as for a full collar, but if the trace loops come very low against the legs, cross them over the back instead of twisting them up.

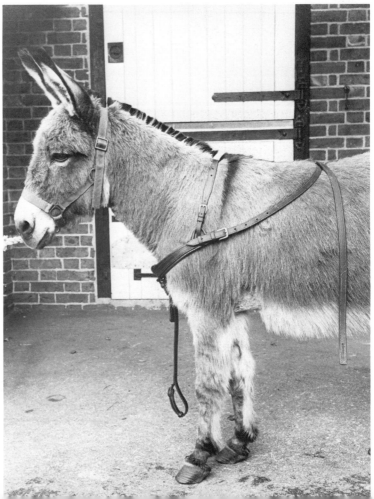

Pad with crupper buckling to back band

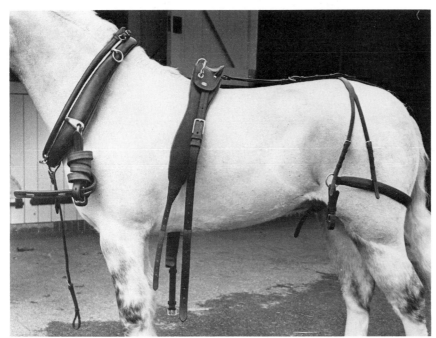

Put the pad on the back, in position. Place the breeching over the back, with the crupper lying free on top of the tail.

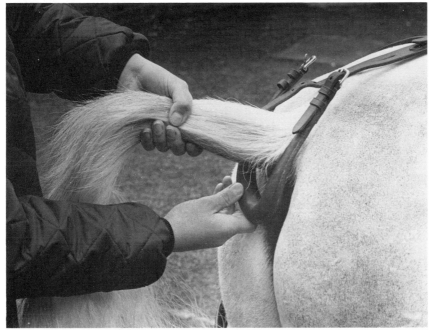

Hold the tail in the left hand, smoothing the hairs down. Slip the free end of the padded crupper under the tail and buckle into position.

Fasten the girth, threading it through the breast plate loop if used. Check for tightness by slipping a hand underneath.

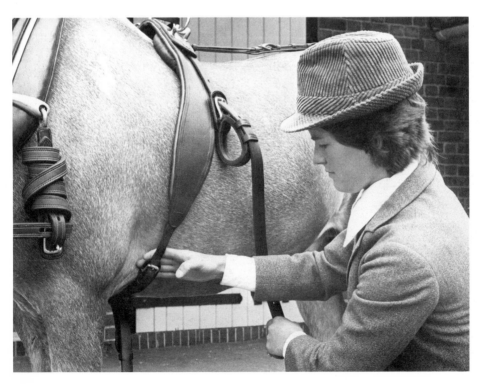

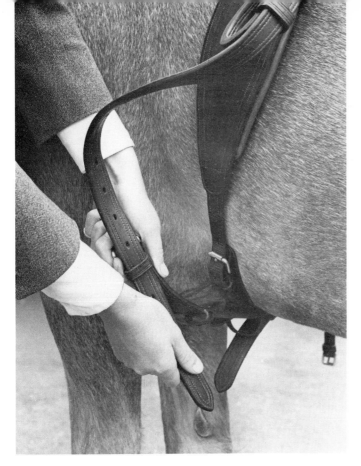

Slip the belly band strap into the keeper, or point, hole to prevent it dragging or banging against the leg.

Pad with fixed crupper

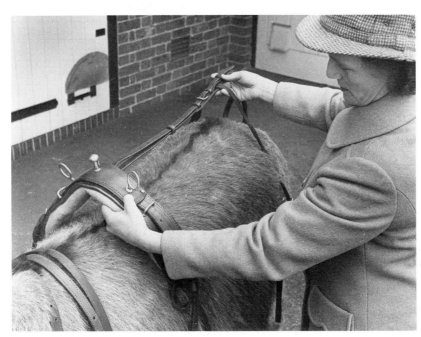

Place the pad on the back about 6in. behind the correct position. Lay the breeching over the back.

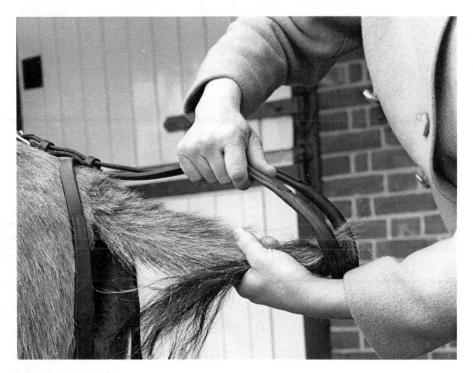

Take the tail in the left hand, doubling up the free end, and slip the crupper over the dock. Smooth the hairs at the top of the dock and push the crupper up into place.

Lift the pad clear of the back and place it forward into its correct position.

Fasten the girth and belly band as shown on page 14.

Reins

Thread the reins through the pad and collar terrets, making sure the buckle of the rein is on the outside. Loop up the long end onto the pad terret, or over the back immediately behind the pad, tucking it under the back strap.

(With a breast collar, with a light 'trotting' neck strap, which has no terrets, thread the reins under the neck strap.)

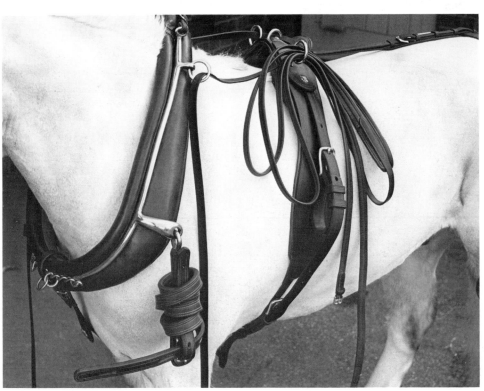

Bridle

Remove the headcollar. Slip the bit into the mouth with the left hand, open the mouth by inserting thumb at the side. Avoid knocking or forcing the bit against the teeth.

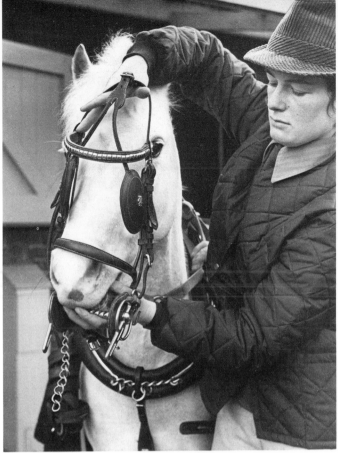

Ease the head piece over the head and ears. Take great care with a donkey's ears. Hold them forward with the right hand and slip them through the head straps.

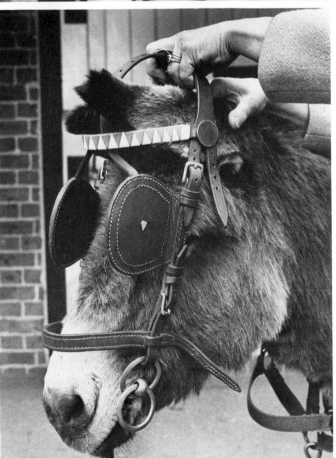

If a donkey will not allow its ears to be touched, use a bridle with a buckled head piece.

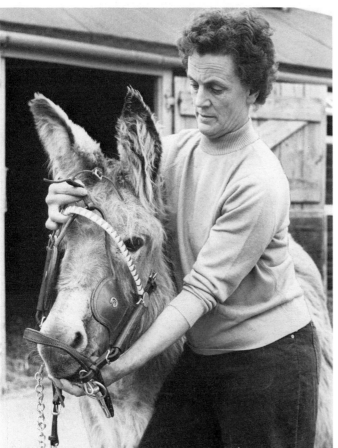

Free the winker stay strap. Put the bit into the mouth, and pass the head piece behind the ears without touching them.

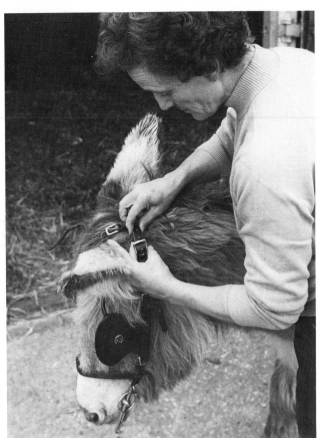

Fasten the buckle of the head piece and re-fasten the stay strap.

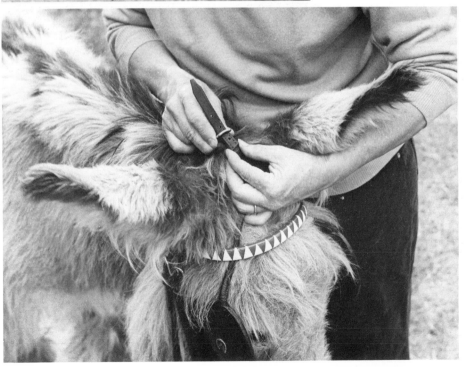

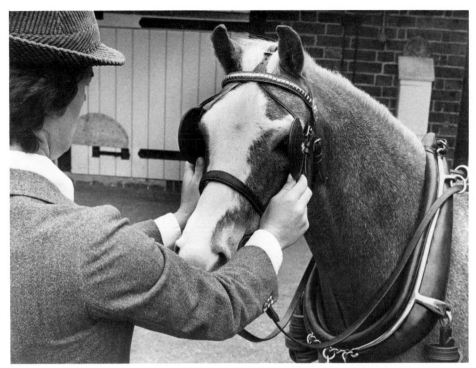

Check that the winkers are in the correct position. The eyes should be central, and the winker stay strap not too tight or loose.

Fasten the throat lash.

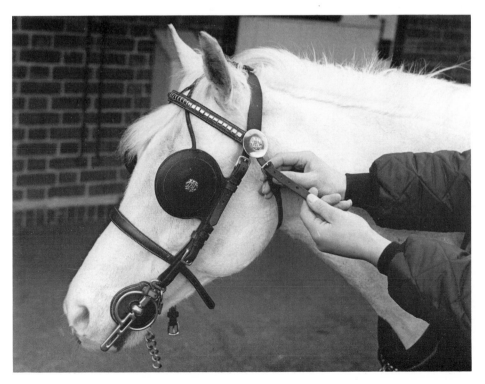

Fasten the nose band.

Fasten the curb chain of the Liverpool bit. Twist the chain clock-wise until absolutely flat. It should not be too tight.

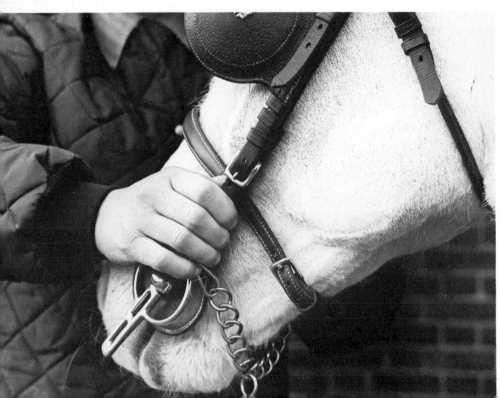

Fasten the reins onto the bit.
  A Liverpool bit, smooth cheek.

A Liverpool bit, rough cheek.

A Liverpool bit, middle bar.

A Wilson snaffle. The reins should always be fastened on both rings. The cheek strap goes on the single, free ring only.

Pony standing complete and ready to put to.
Donkey standing complete and ready to put to.

Putting to

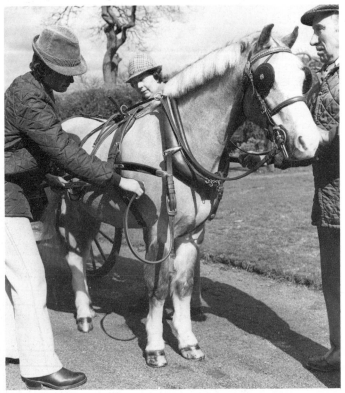

Bring the vehicle up to the animal and slip the shafts into the tugs. Never back the pony into the shafts.

Unloop and thread the traces inside the belly band and hook up both sides.

Fasten the breeching straps on both sides. With a short strap and the D on the outside of the shafts, put the strap round the shaft once, including the trace within the strap.

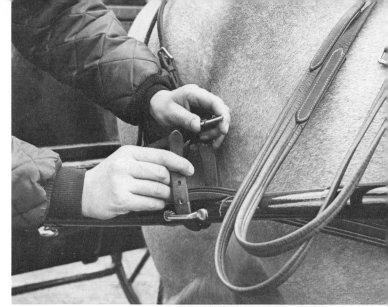

If the vehicle has the D under the shaft, the strap is taken under and through the D. The trace then lies above the breeching straps.

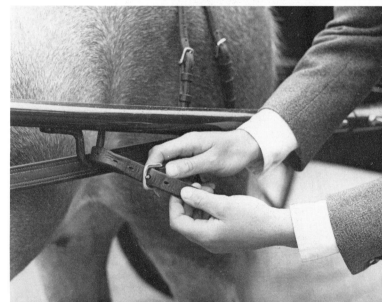

With a longer strap make a figure of eight round the shaft, with the traces within one loop only.

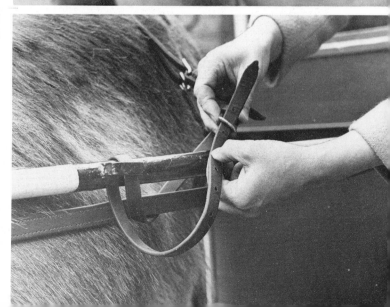

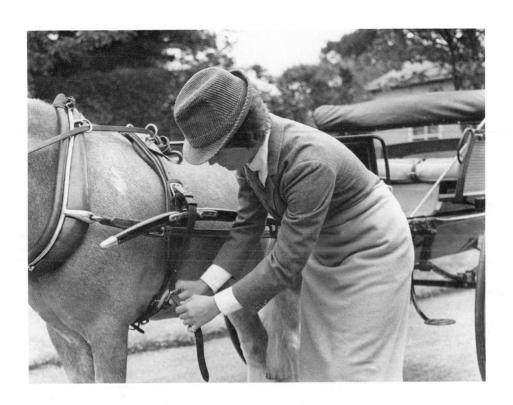

Fasten and adjust the belly band.
    Check the tugs, or shafts, for correct height.

Pony correct and ready

Donkey correct and ready

To take out and un-harness the whole procedure should be reversed exactly. Take care to replace the reins on the pad before unfastening any straps.

The vehicle should be taken back away from the animal, never lead forward out of the shafts. NEVER remove the bridle whilst the animal is in the shafts.

Compiled with the co-operation of:-
MARDONS MR. MIDSHIPMAN EASY
LONGFIELDS' PRINCE CHARMING
and
PETRA OF WOLFHALL
assisted by Caroline Douglas and Jane Dod.

Care of harness

Harness should be cleaned with good saddle soap and rinsed with warm water to remove all dirt and sweat. If possible, with show harness, this should be done on the show ground before packing it up to take it home.

Hang the harness on its racks to allow it to dry thoroughly.

To clean and polish, first take the harness apart, taking care not to lose small pieces such as the keepers from the crupper and bridle.

Before starting to polish make sure the harness is really free from grease. If you have to wash and saddle soap it again, allow it to dry thoroughly before applying the polish. Use a clean brush to apply black (or brown) ABC harness polish to all the leather parts. Proper harness polish is better than boot polish as it feeds the leather. Use neutral Meltonian shoe cream on the patent leather, applied with a soft cloth, not a brush. Work the polish well into the leather, and then apply brass polish to all the metal furniture, taking care not to get it onto the leather. It is a good idea to soak small squares of rag or gamgee, from which the gauze has been removed, in the brass polish and keep it in an airtight tin; this makes application much easier and less messy.

If possible leave the harness in pieces on a bench overnight, in a warm room. This allows the polish to soak into the leather and makes it easier to get a good shine when it is finally brushed.

For the final polishing you need clean brushes which are kept for this job and never used for anything else. Black and brown brushes must be kept separate. You also need several good soft dusters and at least two wash leathers. Old toothbrushes are useful for removing brass polish from initials and crests.

Thoroughly polish all the leather with the brushes first, then with a soft duster and finishing with a wash leather to give the final shine. Patent leather should be polished first with a duster and then the wash leather. If a cloth is used to polish the brass furniture take great care not to break the fragile parts of the crests and initials. A leather is safer for the job.

Reassemble the harness. Packing the harness for a show is a simple and easy job if it is kept in green baize bags marked with the name of the horse to whom it belongs and the piece of harness contained.

For white or cream horses polish the underside of the harness with white cream. Black or brown polish will colour the animals' coats if they sweat.

Care of Cleaning Tools

Cleaning tools should be washed after use. Wash the brushes in detergent, rinse them in cold water and dry them away from direct heat. Wash the leathers in warm water with soap flakes to which a tablespoonful of olive oil has been added. Do not rinse out the soap. Hang the leathers out to dry, occasionally rubbing them to soften them. Treated in this way they will last for years.